We Do

DISCARDED

D056554?

ATTENTION

BUILDING HOURS
FRI 8:00AM to 8:00
12:00PM to 4:00
SUNDAYS CLOSED

21 Day Loan

We Do

A Celebration of Gay and Lesbian Marriage

FOREWORD BY
Gavin Newsom

EDITED BY
Amy Rennert

CHRONICLE BOOKS
SAN FRANCISCO

Page 1: Siddiqi Ray gets
a lift from her new spouse,
Liz McElhinney, outside San
Francisco's City Hall after taking
their wedding vows.

Pages 2–3: A happy couple
waves their marriage license.

Right: A couple embraces on the
steps inside City Hall.

Copyright © 2004. Individual
components of this book are
copyrighted to individual photographers
and authors as indicated on page 143.
Page 143 constitutes a continuation of
the copyright page.

All rights reserved. No part of this book
may be reproduced in any form without
written permission from the publisher.

Library of Congress Cataloging-in-
Publication Data available.

ISBN 0-8118-4612-1

Manufactured in Canada.

Designed by Dennis Gallagher and
John Sullivan, Visual Strategies.

Distributed in Canada by
Raincoast Books
9050 Shaughnessy Street
Vancouver, British Columbia V6P 6E5

10 9 8 7 6 5 4 3 2 1

Chronicle Books LLC
85 Second Street
San Francisco, California 94105

www.chroniclebooks.com

Foreword

By Gavin Newsom, Mayor of San Francisco

Growing up in an Irish-Catholic household in San Francisco, I was taught that a loving commitment between two people was the foundation of a strong marriage. I was also taught that discrimination was wrong. Today, as a married man, I enjoy with my wife 1,049 legal rights, such as hospital visitation, shared health coverage, and retirement benefits. More important, my wife and I enjoy the dignity, respect, and affirmation of our relationship that comes with being a married couple. However, these same rights have historically been denied to other committed couples, solely on the basis of their gender.

All this changed when I directed San Francisco County Clerk Nancy Alfaro to make marriage available to *all* loving, committed couples who applied for a license. I acted in order to honor my upbringing and my own marriage, support the commitment of real couples to form lifelong bonds, and defend the oath I took as mayor to protect liberty and justice for all, not just those of a certain class. I refused to deny to any person the right to make this deeply personal commitment to another human being, and to publicly celebrate that commitment to fidelity, intimacy, companionship, and family.

This beautiful book shows how the historic weddings performed in City Hall between February 12 and March 11, 2004, were about far more than philosophical or legal principles. They were about real people, like San Francisco couple Del Martin and Phyllis Lyon, who have shared a loving, committed relationship for fifty-one years with none of the same protections granted opposite-sex couples. They were about the hundreds of same-sex couples who waited overnight in the rain on the sidewalk outside City Hall for a marriage license. They were also about the goodness of complete strangers who brought coffee and blankets to the couples standing outside in the cold, and others who anonymously sent countless dozens of roses to "the happy couple" awaiting a marriage license, in honor of gay relatives or partners who couldn't make the journey.

On February 12, 2004, when San Francisco Mayor Gavin Newsom, left, instructed city officials to issue marriage licenses to same-sex couples, gay community leaders Phyllis Lyon, center, and Del Martin became the first gay couple to wed.

As you'll see in this book, it was a special time in San Francisco. You could feel the energy, excitement, and enthusiasm of those who came from around the world to be married. They were met with cheers, as well as tears of joy, as they emerged from the County Clerk's office, marriage licenses in hand, to take their vows and exchange rings on the grand staircase and throughout City Hall. It is a familiar wedding scene long enjoyed by opposite-sex couples. For twenty-nine days it was enjoyed by all. I trust that it will be again.

Introduction

By Amy Rennert

For twenty-nine days in the winter of 2004, San Francisco's City Hall was transformed. Joyous couples from forty-six states and eight other countries pledged to love and comfort each other for the rest of their lives. The outpouring of support from family, friends, colleagues, and volunteers was unprecedented.

My partner, Louise, and I were one of the lucky 4,037 couples to wed. We've been faithfully together for seventeen years, in sickness and in health, for richer, for poorer, for better, for worse. I use those words—spoken for generations—because they were part of our wedding vows and ritual that had more power than I'd imagined possible. We'd never had a commitment ceremony, and we didn't believe our relationship needed outside validation. But everything changed when Gavin Newsom, San Francisco's thirty-six-year-old straight married Irish Catholic mayor, made these extraordinary days possible.

Shanna Holladay, left, shares a laugh with newlywed spouse Jennifer Sells, as their son, Evan, looks on.

It all felt so right—it was personal but also political and so much bigger than the two of us; a deeply moving moment. For us and for so many other newlyweds it was, and is, a matter of love and a matter of rights.

We Do is a celebratory book, one that captures this historic time and tells the human story. It began with a surprising and courageous decision by a new mayor; appropriately, he has written the foreword.

In the opening pages, we showcase the first of these historic nuptials: Phyllis Lyon, 79, and Del Martin, 83. Activists and partners for more than half a century, they were ready to make it official when the call came from the mayor's office less than a day earlier.

It was the news of their wedding and the eighty-nine others on February 12 that inspired and motivated thousands of other proposals and trips to City Hall. Hundreds of straight and gay volunteers joined the celebration, and the gilded doors of the beaux arts building swung open repeatedly while one elated married couple after another emerged to shouts, cheers, and car horns all through Valentine's Day and the holiday weekend.

Most of the couples who obtained marriage licenses in San Francisco live in California. The couple in line behind us drove from Sacramento with their two young children twice in three days because, after a ten-hour wait on Saturday, they had yet to make it inside. Tired and determined, they then showed up at 3 a.m. and waited patiently for their turn, as did countless others. Never before has standing in line felt so good or led to so many friendships and shared anniversaries. Some waited overnight in the cold and rain, so strong was their desire to make a lifetime commitment official.

As the days turned into weeks, City Hall eventually required applicants to make appointments, and the lines disappeared. People had more time to prepare and invite others to join them. I found myself returning time and again, sometimes as a witness for friends and sometimes because I just couldn't stay away from the joy and love and history in the making.

History may have started in San Francisco, but it didn't stay just there. Same-sex weddings followed in Oregon, New York, New Mexico, and New Jersey, and we've included images of those as well.

We've set up this book so that you'll experience the wedding day the way the early couples did—first the long lines and camaraderie outside and inside City Hall, then the filling out of forms, followed by the weddings throughout the building. There are a few quiet moments in between, and then finally, there are the triumphal exits from City Hall. At the end of the book are scenes from some of the festivities that followed the weddings in a grand reception for newlyweds.

For those who were there, this book will forever be a keepsake. For everyone else, I hope *We Do* will be a reminder that true love is worth fighting for.

A couple greets the crowd outside City Hall.

In February, two days before Valentine's Day, Del Martin, 83, in a purple pants suit, and Phyllis Lyon, 79, in a blue one, slipped quietly into City Hall. So did witnesses Kate Kendell and Roberta Achtenberg, as well as a handful of mayoral aides. Few others knew what was about to take place inside the assessor's office.

Del and Phyllis, days before their fifty-first anniversary, were the first gay couple to be married in Mabel Teng's office at City Hall. In the background, from far left, are Kate Kendell, Executive Director of the National Center for Lesbian Rights, Roberta Achtenberg, Senior Vice President of the San Francisco Chamber of Commerce, and members of Mayor Gavin Newsom's staff: Joe Caruso, Director of Neighborhood Services, Steve Kawa, Chief of Staff, and Joyce Newstat, Director of Policy.

Above, Del Martin and soon-to-be-legal spouse Phyllis Lyon wait for the formalities to begin. At right, Del supervises as Phyllis fills in the requisite application forms for their marriage license. In all, ninety gay and lesbian couples would tie the knot on the first day of same-sex weddings.

"I felt the weight of history in a way I've never felt before. It is remarkable and profound."

–Kate Kendell, executive director, National Center for Lesbian Rights

City Assessor/Recorder Mabel Teng officiates.

Phyllis and Del hold aloft their marriage certificate outside City Hall.

Four days after Mayor Gavin Newsom directed city officials to begin issuing marriage licenses to gay and lesbian couples, the line of applicants wrapped around San Francisco's City Hall and into surrounding streets.

Robin Baugh, left, and
Maria Jones spent the night
lined up in the rain.

"The line Monday wound for three blocks near the ornate City Hall, with shish kebabs, umbrellas, doughnuts, coffee, and even breath mints being shared."

—Harriet Chiang, *San Francisco Chronicle*

The pouring rain did nothing to dampen the enthusiasm of San Franciscans Lisa Inman and Alisa Gilden. They spent the night in line on the steps of City Hall with Ilana Drummond and Sharon Dulberg.

At closing time on February 15, couples were told to come back the next day on a first-come, first-served basis. Rather than leave, they formed the line for the next day immediately and spent the night.

Despite the wet weather and cold temperatures, applicants like Persephone Gonzalez, left, and Delia Meraz, both from Long Beach, California, showed patience and good humor throughout the wait.

"Wearing tuxedos and lacy bridal gowns, sweatshirts and sneakers, they have camped out on the sidewalks for days waiting their turn, forging friendships as they tried to ignore drenching rains."

–Harriet Chiang, *San Francisco Chronicle*

Couples and volunteers mingle in the rotunda of San Francisco's City Hall.

Dr. Davina Kotulski, left, and Molly McKay, Executive Director of Marriage Equality California, pass through metal detectors at City Hall on their way to be married.

Supervisor Bevan Dufty, left, and
other volunteers who were deputized
to officiate at weddings have a quiet
moment on City Hall's grand staircase.

Entering City Hall.

It took James Harker, front left, and Paul Festa nearly two hours to reach the door to apply for a marriage license.

"We waited in line for over ten hours. . . . How often do you get a bunch of strangers together, put them in a long line in bad weather, and everyone is laughing and joyous?"

—Andrea Bourguet, newlywed

"It was, of course, just more of an eye-opener how much love there was in that long, long line. This is all about love, and love will win out."

–Reverend Alexandra True,
Marriage Equality
California chapter leader

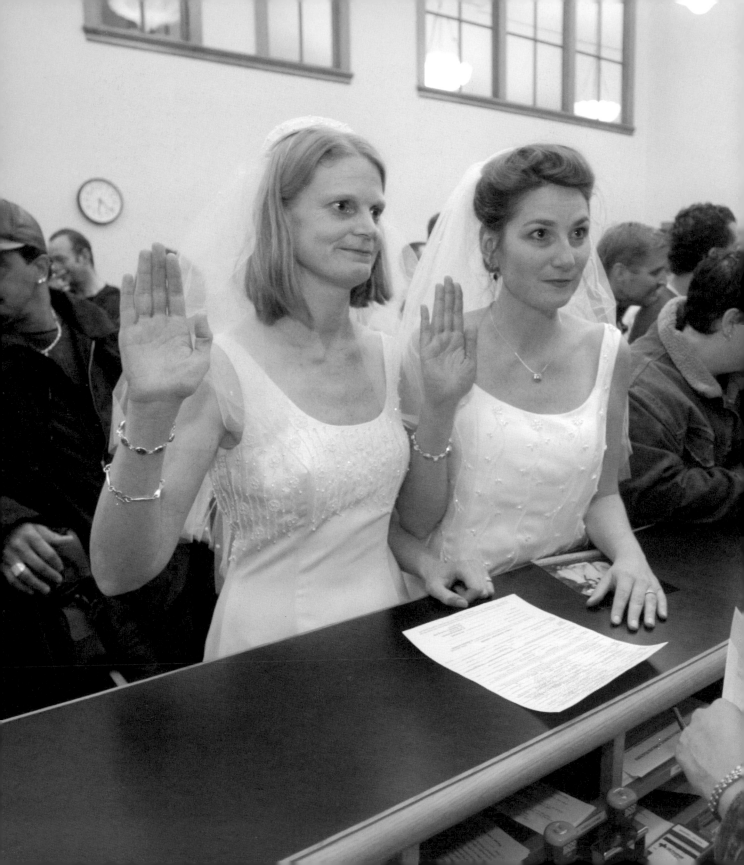

The line outside the
doors of the county
clerk's office.

Cissie Bonini, left,
and Lora Pertle are
sworn in before
their ceremony.

"Happily legal after seventeen years. . ."

–Peter Ginsberg,
newlywed

Gary Levinson, left, and Peter Ginsberg
in the county clerk's office.

Liz Pesch, left, and Nikki Raeburn kiss
their five-year-old son, Joshua. The couple
made two trips to City Hall in the same
day—first to get the license and then to
get married.

San Franciscans Andrew Nance,
left, and Jim Maloney take their vows.
Leonardo Montenegro is their witness.

"Being married there was like a dream."

–Sher Strugnell, newlywed

Photographer Anna Kuperberg and Carla Johnson were married by friend Beth Grossman, who performed the Jewish ceremony under a *chuppah* (canopy) in the South Gallery of City Hall's fourth floor.

Being married
in City Hall
was especially
meaningful to
Carla, left, who,
as a carpenter,
helped repair
the building
after it was
damaged in
the 1989
earthquake.
Anna is at right.

Anna and
Carla shared
the duties of
smashing the
linen-wrapped
wineglass.

Andrea Bourguet, left, and Jennifer Nannini met through friends over fourteen years ago while in college in Southern California.

Susan Lowenberg, left, and Joyce Newstat were married in the mayor's office with Mayor Gavin Newsom officiating.

Frank Capley, left, and Joe Alfano.

Calvin Crosby, left, and Jean Taylor-Woodbury spent thirteen years together and sixteen hours in line before getting married, but say it was "so worth the wait."

41

"The building's grand staircase was so jammed with couples, witnesses, lilies, and deputy wedding commissioners that it was hard to tell where one wedding party stopped and the next began."

–Harriet Chiang, *San Francisco Chronicle*

Rachel Lanzerotti, left, and Carol Cantwell
kiss at the end of their wedding ceremony.

A couple takes their vows surrounded by
friends and family.

In March, Multnomah County, Oregon, began issuing same-sex marriage licenses. By the end of that first day, almost four hundred joyous gay couples from all over Oregon and Washington had acquired licenses, and seventy-five were wed.

Terri Harvath, far right, of Portland, was among the first to line up outside the Multnomah County offices in Portland.

Janine Zeler Lane, left, married Karen, with Karen's seven-year-old daughter, Delancey, and family members Todd and Ruth Adkins looking on as witnesses.

Sara Graham and
Bonnie Tinker were
one of the first couples
to receive a marriage
license.

Marilyn Walker, far left,
her partner, Claudia
Keith, and two friends
wait in line at the
Multnomah County
offices. Both couples
married that week.

In New Mexico's Sandoval County, sixty-six same-sex marriage licenses were issued in February. Wedding ceremonies took place in the street outside the courthouse in Bernalillo and outside the capitol building in Santa Fe.

Beth Saltzman, left, and Patti Levey were united in a group ceremony.

As Reverend Peter Denlea, center, watches, Dennis and Charles Enyart-Tucker exchange wedding rings.

*I*n February, Mayor Jason West of New Paltz, New York, officiated at the weddings of twenty-five same-sex marriages. In Asbury Park, New Jersey, licenses were issued in March.

Major Jeffrey McGowan, left, and Billiam van Roestenberg celebrate after being married by New Paltz Mayor Jason West on February 27.

On March 8, Louis Navarrete, left, and Ric Best became the first same-sex couple to be married in New Jersey. Deputy Mayor James Bruno performed the ceremony.

Jeff Karliner, left, and Henry Johnson (off camera) show off the wedding bands Jeff made for them twenty-nine years ago. Until the two were married in New Paltz, the rings had never been worn.

Alice Dodd, left, and Jillian Armenante
(actresses on the television series
Judging Amy) adjust one another's bridal
veils and make a few calls to friends and
family after getting married. They drove
up from Los Angeles for the occasion.

Chris Ruff and Peter Van Dyne flew from Anchorage, Alaska, to San Francisco to take their vows.

"We didn't have to discuss getting married at City Hall. We just did it. It wasn't about politics, or the civil disobedience, or the social activism. . . . It was about our love for each other and our love for family."

—Eric Zing, newlywed

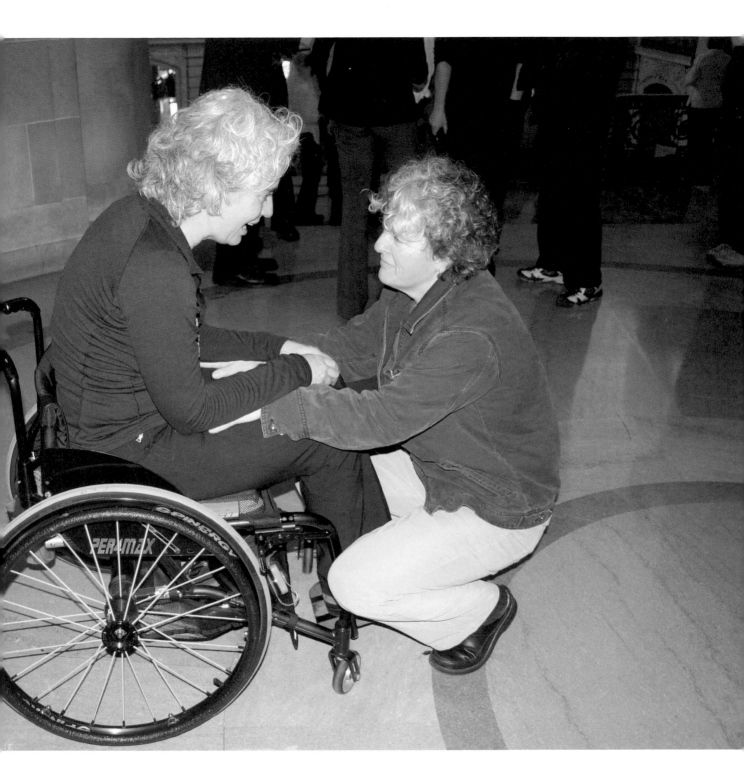

Two men clasp
hands as they
recite their
wedding vows
in City Hall.

On Valentine's Day, their
fifteenth anniversary, Maureen
Anderson, left, and Susan
Colson celebrated by getting
married. Daughters Delia
(between her parents) and
Zoe, far right, look on.

Mike Farrah, senior advisor
to the mayor, signed off on
one of the happy couples
he married.

Lenora Gevock, left, and
Jennifer Stock of Oakland
exchange rings.

Angela Hackenschmidt,
left, and Patricia Hageny.

Michelle Baird, left, and
Susan Doughty were the
777th couple to be married.

"It was less about the ceremony than it was about the girls, in hopes that this would somehow make their own future more secure. I know I'll be with Eric for life; I've known that since I met him."

—Doug Okun, newlywed

Eric Ethington, center, exchanges vows with Doug Okun, right, while holding their twin daughters, Sophia Rose and Elizabeth Ruby.

Bill Mitchell, left, and
David Stocks came
from Los Angeles
to be married at
City Hall. They met
ballroom dancing.

Writers Pat Holt, left,
and Terry Ryan, together
for over twenty years,
resolved to make it
twenty more.

After seventeen years
together, Amy Rennert, left,
and Louise Kollenbaum
were married February 17.

For many applicants, including these two who flew in from Hawaii, waiting in line turned into spontaneous engagement parties, making the eventual ceremony all the sweeter.

"It's time to honor and celebrate all those who seek to strengthen the human family."

–Reverend Alan Jones,
Dean of Grace Cathedral,
San Francisco

California State Assemblyman Mark Leno, right, officiates at the wedding of two men, children in tow.

California Assemblywoman Carole Migden, top, presides over the wedding of Nanci Clarence, left, and Lidia Szajko in the City Hall rotunda. This took place just before her own marriage to her longtime partner, Chris Arguedas.

"Supervisor Bevan Dufty asked us to take our vows. We did so as if this were the most natural thing in the world to be doing on this particular Thursday afternoon. And it was. I do. I do. I will. I will."

—William D. Glenn, newlywed

Supervisor Tom Ammiano, left, marries Oren Slozberg and Irwin Keller, who described the ceremony as "fast, to the point, and very romantic."

Volunteer Bill Jones, center, performed more ceremonies than anyone else—457.

After flying in from Philadelphia, Lauren Himmel, left, and Denise Ramzy, right, celebrate with Liza Sibley, who conducted the ceremony.

"We were waiting to be paired with an official and take the final plunge, when a volunteer approached us and asked if we wanted flowers for our ceremony. Flowers were a luxury we hadn't allowed ourselves, what with all the waiting and uncertainty of the day. She said they were being sent in from all over the country. Confused, I asked who they were for. 'They're for you!' she said. Complete strangers sending flowers to show support for what we were about to do . . . incredible. We picked out a beautiful bouquet of lilac roses and tulips. There was a card attached that said: 'To a Loving Couple: Best wishes for a long and happy life together. Congratulations on your marriage. Bruce and Sue, Atlanta PFLAG.' The card is going right next to the marriage certificate in the album."

—Jennifer Nannini, newlywed

"We just spent the time looking into each other's eyes and placing the rings on each other's fingers. Then it was over. She said, 'I now pronounce you spouses for life,' and we just kissed and cried."

—Janet Thomson, newlywed

Yesenia Renteria, left, and Norma Listman captured in a private moment by photographer Jules Greenberg.

Friends of Yesenia
and Norma created a
spontaneous keepsake of
their good wishes, right.

Your Love has affected us all in the most beautiful way imaginable. Your friends and family are a reflection of that. We love you very much. Matt & Aaron

Love and happiness. Always. Bexito & Sara

con todo mi amor —
tus espíritus brillan
y me hacen brillar
Que gusto ser miembro
de tu familia tan hermosa
Siempre
Stefani

"And then you know....
Life is Beautiful...."
♥ Elizabeth (and Fred!)

Let love shine as brightly as your smiles... & congrats!
with love & Gina. Toyzawa

Здравие, спекку и ауг моивоu / gglose mean love

Yesenia y Norma
Las quiero mucho
Con toda mi alma
Les deseo lo mejor
en la vida siempre.
Con cariño su
amiga siempre
Klaudia

Blessings y más Blessings
Y todavía más Blessings
ahora Y siempre...
♥ Cynthia

You Both are so beautiful and blessed.
Thank you for stepping together with pride to declare your civil right to love. Dixie

Happy 4U Norma you are so bright! Let your light that shines! You a STAR!

Yesica! I am so light & bright Best wishes David

Peace + Love + Happiness Always. Very big congratulations! Tim

It's days like this when you know everything's right in the universe. I love you both. Teri ☺

To the most beautiful girls in the world! Thank you so much & lifting me Shine in this. Steph you & amazing day. Because you are a love! I will always be & Julio

Your love and pride spreads Happiness into our world and with that I hope to give the two of you equal love and a life time of Happiness!! Besos Julio

[Arabic text]

2-27-04 @ 6:35 P.M. Yessica, Hermanita, Felicidades en tu gran día. Tienen mi soporte por vida Sinceramente Yanis

J.R. 27/08/04
¡Ys de sus todas su felicidad!
Ti, Cynthia La X xx

— Julep green bar
Yesi + Norma — Everlasting love and companionship. Love, Andrea

may all your days be filled with love. Moustafa&lulu

Meant for each other! Happy forever Ashley Ed.

Gracias por la lucha!! Esto les convierte en luchadoras. Con toda la dicha A Esperanza
Eternamente Yesenia
Les deseo amor siempre.
Vickie

Que juntas se rían de la vida simpre. — L.E.A.

May you both be blessed with lifelong Joy & Happiness. With love & Friendship, Bethany

♥ Yesenia and Norma — Friendship, Passion and Laughter... You have it all! I love you both. Jamie

Full of laughter Full of love Forever ♥ Tim

Paint the world with your love ....
Con Cariños, La Estrellita ★

Hoy, Mañana, Siempre puro

♥ Rosa

to eternal "devotion" and wild, inspiring love ♥ Julee

YESI & NORMA WHEN I LOOK AT YOUR PICTURE I JUST WANT TO SMILE. BE HAPPY! ALAN!

"I feel like she is my other half.
She's my puzzle piece. I'm in
this for good. You know, I can't
imagine life without her."

—Kelli Carpenter-O'Donnell, newlywed

Rosie O'Donnell and her longtime
partner, Kelli Carpenter-O'Donnell,
left, speak from the heart after
being married by San Francisco
City Treasurer Susan Leal, shown
on the second stair.

Joe Lazzaro, left, held hands with his partner of ten years, former air force fighter pilot David Knight, as Donald Bird presided at their City Hall wedding.

Diane Ferro, left, and
Mary Veronica Palmer of
Shasta County, California.

Alameda, California, residents Thomas Bullen, left, and Roger Koopmann have been together for twenty-one years.

We are gathered here in the presence of witnesses for the purpose of uniting in matrimony

_____ and _____

The contract of marriage is most solemn and is not to be entered into lightly, but thoughtfully and seriously with a deep realization of its obligations and responsibilities.

Please remember that love, loyalty and understanding are the foundations of a happy and enduring home.

No other human ties are more tender and no other vows more important than those you are about to pledge.

Please face each other and join hands.

Do you _____, take _____ to be your spouse for life? (repeat)

Do you promise to love and comfort each other, honor and keep each other in sickness and in health, for richer and for poorer, for better or for worse and be faithful to each other as long as you both shall live.

RING CEREMONY- _____place the ring on _____'s finger and repeat after me to him/her

I give you this ring in token and pledge of my constant faith and abiding love. With this ring, I thee wed. (repeat)

Now that you have joined yourselves in matrimony, may you strive all your lives to meet this commitment with the same love and devotion you now possess.

By virtue of the authority vested in me by the State of California, I now pronounce you

_____ and _____spouses for life.

Officials most often used these wedding vows.

"When we had our commitment ceremony seven years ago, Gwen's parents weren't ready to give us their wholehearted support. Our City Hall wedding gave them a second chance to come through for us and they showed up unexpectedly . . . It meant more than we can ever say."

—Jessica Beebe, newlywed

Count the two of us, long married, among the sentimental spectators who reaffirmed romance with a visit to City Hall this weekend. We stood in the sidewalk throng, beaming and at the same time blinking away tears, applauding newlyweds as they skipped down the steps of City Hall.

Amen to the instant "ministers," their stick-on labels sufficient stand-ins for robes of office; congratulations to the mother who was overheard on Valentine's Day telling her toddler son, "I'm marrying mommy...we'll explain later." Bon appétit to Abby Stepnitz, Emily Cohen, and Ryan McDonald O'Lear, three University of San Francisco students who had pooled their resources to buy wedding cakes that they sliced and handed out to the just-married; and a clap on the back to the father of one bride, who upon gazing joyfully at his daughter, her spouse, and their children, proclaimed, "I am proud to be a San Franciscan."

Many dates in local history mark tragedy: earthquake, fire, assassination. But from here on in—no matter what the courts decide—San Franciscans will mark these special days in February with big red hearts.

—Leah Garchik,
San Francisco Chronicle

Jenna Smith, left, kicks up
her heels after receiving
her marriage license with
Jennifer Franet.

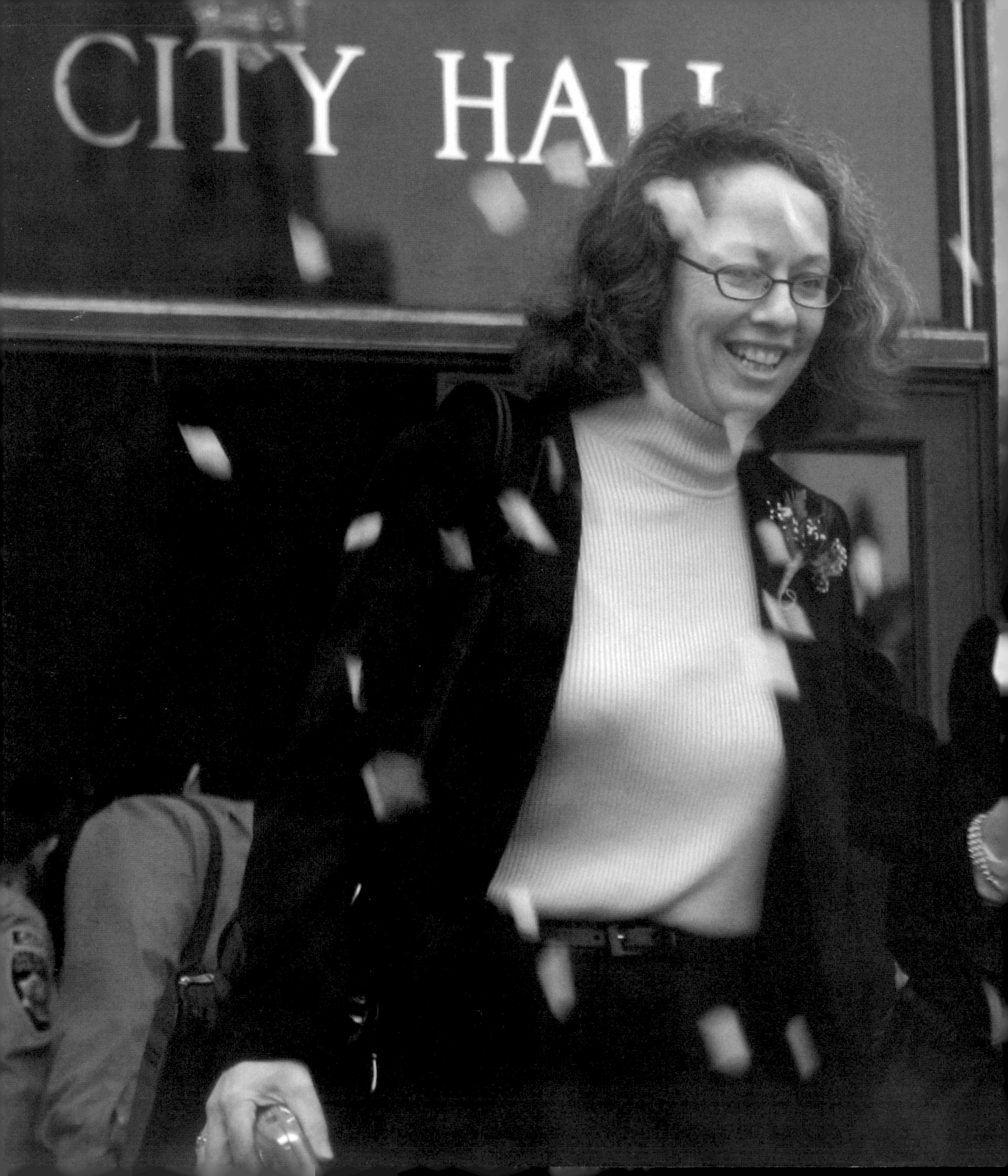
CITY HAL

"This is the

happiest place

on earth."

—Mabel Teng,
San Francisco
Assessor/Recorder

Following their ceremonies,
each couple found their own
way of exiting City Hall.

"...*the feeling of joy was overwelming.*"

–Derek Powazek, photographer

Machu Latorre, left, and Paige
Fratesi stand in front of San
Francisco City Hall with their
marriage license.

"What's happening in San Francisco is the sexiest thing to happen to marriage in years."

–Armistead Maupin,
author of *Tales of the City*.

Georjina Graciano, left,
and Maria Castillo dance
in front of a mariachi
band at City Hall after
their wedding ceremony.

Brett Mangels, left, and
Tanya Neiman went to
City Hall for history and
politics, but were "delighted
that marriage managed to
deepen our commitment of
twenty-one years."

Cynthia Rickert, left,
and Michie Wong
share a kiss.

"As to what happens legally and politically down the road, it won't change that moment for us. I'd already wanted to spend the rest of my life with Janet."

—Jamye Ford, newlywed

Paola Quinones, left, and Anne Rosendin pause for a wedding portrait.

San Franciscans Janet Thomson, left, and Jamye Ford outside City Hall.

Leah Brooks, left, and Barbara Tannenbaum both wore jewelry inherited from their mothers.

It was impossible for newlyweds not to notice the applause and cheers coming from the crowds outside City Hall. Deborah, left, and Kim clasped hands and waved at the legion of new friends awaiting them.

"Leah and I have registered three times as domestic partners, beginning in 1991. We bought a home together. We intertwined our lives with those of our families through the many birthdays, holidays, bar mitzvahs, and funerals that have taken place in two decades. As our ten-year-old niece said, 'Aren't Barb and Leah married already?' The answer, as I was about to learn, was both yes and no."

–Barbara Tannenbaum, newlywed

"Even though we've been together for twelve years, we weren't prepared for the level of emotion we felt when we received the license. It was the most important day in our lives and a day that will shape history."

—Calla Devlin, newlywed

Shera Penner and
Amy Martin flew in from
Salt Lake City, Utah.

A couple dances
down the steps of
City Hall.

Paul Donnelly, left, and Daniel Navarro first stood in line for seven hours in an unsuccessful attempt to marry, then made an appointment for a week later.

San Jose police officer Jincy Pace, left,
and Beach Sachse, both West Point
graduates, display their marriage license.

Anil Dutt, left, and Randy Ynegas.

Sandra Hollingsworth, left,
and Robyn Lock.

The San Francisco Gay Men's Chorus serenaded couples with "Going to the Chapel," among other songs.

"It has also boosted the neighborhood's sense of community, turning its streets into one big wedding reception. Many newlyweds head straight from the Civic Center down Market Street to the Castro, driving convertibles emblazoned with 'Just Married,' wearing bridal gowns and tuxes, and waving their new marriage licenses."

—Heather Knight, *San Francisco Chronicle*

"For our wedding lunch, Bill and I went directly to In-N-Out Burger and had double cheeseburgers, shared a basket of fries, and I had a forbidden chocolate shake. The whole blessed day was both graced and utterly unremarkable."

—Scott Hafner, newlywed

David Latulippe and Ronn Seely showed up on Valentine's Day to be married, blender in hand.

Outside City Hall, Susan Croy and Stevie Van Emmenis danced on the lawn, then checked out their moves with photographer Margot Duane, below.

Bonnie Feinberg, Carol Cantwell,
Rachel Lanzerotti, Beth Freedman,
Randy Sweringen, Michael Mansfield,
Charles Haletky, Jenny Caughey,
Andrew Sullivan, and Alicia Chazen
toasted the recent newlyweds.

On February 22, a wedding reception was held at the Hyatt Regency Grand Ballroom in San Francisco in honor of Del Martin and Phyllis Lyon, and all of the other couples that had gotten married. It was a joyous celebration of love, marriage, family, and community, with performances by the Montclair Women's Big Band, Linda Tillery, Vicki Randle, the San Francisco Gay Men's Chorus, and the Lesbian/Gay Chorus of San Francisco. Over two thousand people attended.

"Part political rally, part dance party, part potluck, part traditional wedding reception, complete with cake and toasts and kisses."

–Rona Marech, *San Francisco Chronicle*

Friends toast one another
at the reception held in the
Hyatt Regency ballroom.

Leslie Caccamese, left,
and Deirdre Bourdet.

Nicole, left, and Lorena Aviles-Galberth.

Robert Zivnuska
and John Wang.

Couples posed for more formal portraits at the Hyatt Regency reception.

Jeanne Fong, left, and Jennifer J. Lin.

Heidi Denton, left, and Gaydeen Valdez, with their son, Teddy Valdez-Denton.

Laura, left, and Julie Rosenthal-Bauer, with their daughter, Arielle.

Sue Burish, left, and Jennie Schacht.

Patrick Connors, left, and Rob DeKoch.

Susan Shain, with arms raised,
and Sally McCaffrey celebrate
their recent nuptials.

The celebrations continued in Portland following ceremonies at Keller Auditorium. Tracie Jones, left, and Candice Wicklinder dance after being married on March 3.

Walls are Dancing

"Did you hear that winter's over?"*

Roses open, naked, inviting entry of bees
The sun laughs at darkness.

Love used to hide inside images. No more.

LOVE HAS GONE PUBLIC
OUT IN THE OPEN
Women who love women
Men who love men
Clamor to marry
Leaping through walls,
            Crushing barriers

Nothing can stop the LIGHT
And the greening of this spring

THE ORCHARDS ARE FULL OF FRUIT
We cannot contain them; they burst open, and

            WE FEAST   WE FEAST
            At this banquet of EQUALITY

Nothing CAN STAY BOUND OR IMPRISONED.

THE LINES OF THIS POEM
ESCAPE THE PAGE
AND BECOME THE MUSIC OF YOU

Refrains of love Phyllis, love Del
Even I who worry too much about love,
Look into Cecil's eyes, look into Her Eyes,
all judgement gone.

ONLY LOVE
OCCUPIES THIS SPACE BETWEEN
            OUR HUMAN FLESH.

We are MORE than what we have been
More than gender or sexual orientation —
More whole.
You expand our humanity with the justice
            you seek.
LIGHT RISES,

NOTHING stays repressed
When women's laughter
Pours like the wind spilling wine*
This marriage is history
This marriage is freedom
this marriage is spirit

Listen . . .
The walls are dancing
the walls are dancing

            the walls are crumbling, they are
                    dancing
            they are singing . . .

—Janice Mirikitani
San Francisco Poet Laureate 2000

* lines from Rumi

Phyllis Lyon, center, helps
Del Martin, right, make the
first cut in their wedding
cake, provided by Elizabeth
Falkner of Citizen Cake.

Acknowledgments

Special thanks go to San Francisco Mayor Gavin Newsom and his senior staff, especially Policy Director Joyce Newstat who helped make this book possible; Joe Caruso, Director of Neighborhood Services, who led 287 volunteers during the weddings and answered our questions with great enthusiasm; photographer Daniel Homsey, from the office of Neighborhood Services, who captured more than 1,000 images, many of them featured in this book. Daniel and his wife Catherine volunteered during Valentine's Day weekend, marrying 120 couples in total.

The *We Do* team also thanks Julie Burton and Dena Fischer at The Amy Rennert Agency, Inc.; Kenn Altine, Nanette Bisher, Elizabeth A. Cain, Susan Gilbert, Kathleen Hennessy, and Narda Zacchino at the *San Francisco Chronicle*; Don Bowden of AP/Wide World Photos; Mindy Bosker, president of the Bay Area Community of Women; Janice Mirikitani, Poet Laureate of San Francisco; Thom Lynch, executive director of the LGBT Community Center of San Francisco; David Hamlet of Visual Strategies; and Christina Amini, Barbara Beaver, Shona Bayley, Alicia Bergin, Mikyla Bruder, Andrea Burnett, Calla Devlin, Kendra Kallan, and Jane Steele at Chronicle Books.

Thanks also go to Roberta Achtenberg, James Carroll, Pat Holt, Hildegard Manley, and Ray Souza.

Note: Many people celebrated the weddings pictured in this book, and we have tried our best to properly identify newlyweds, friends, family, officials, and others, gay and straight. Please advise the publisher of any additions or corrections, or incomplete or inaccurate identifications, and we will address them in future printings. All photographs taken in San Francisco unless otherwise indicated. Contact WeDo@chroniclebooks.com, or write to We Do Corrections, Chronicle Books, 85 Second Street, San Francisco, CA 94105.